A Simple Guide
to

Practical books that inspire

Lump Sum Investment
Assess your needs; explore the opportunities; maximise your investments

Reducing Your Tax Bill
A simple guide to paying less personal tax

Saving and Investing
How to achieve financial security and make your money grow

Making Your Money Work for You
How to use simple investment principles to increase your wealth

howtobooks

For full details, please send for a free copy
of the latest catalogue to:

How To Books
3 Newtec Place, Magdalen Road
Oxford OX4 1RE United Kingdom
email: info@howtobooks.co.uk
http://www.howtobooks.co.uk

A Simple Guide to Pensions

*Discover how to solve the pensions puzzle
and provide for a comfortable retirement*

John Claxton

Published by How To Books Ltd,
3 Newtec Place, Magdalen Road,
Oxford OX4 1RE, United Kingdom.
Tel: (01865) 793806. Fax: (01865) 248780
email: info@howtobooks.co.uk
http://www.howtobooks.co.uk

All rights reserved. No part of this work may be reproduced
or stored in an information retrieval system (other than for
purposes of review) without the express permission of the publisher in writing.

© Copyright 2002 John Claxton

First edition 2002

British Library Cataloguing in Publication Data.
A catalogue record for this book is available from the British Library.

Edited by David Kershaw
Cover design by Baseline Arts Ltd, Oxford

Produced for How To Books by Deer Park Productions
Typeset by Kestrel Data, Exeter
Printed and bound by Bell & Bain Ltd, Glasgow

NOTE: The material contained in this book is set out in good faith for general
guidance and no liability can be accepted for loss or expense incurred as a
result of relying in particular circumstances on statements made in this book.
Laws and regulations are complex and liable to change, and readers should
check the current position with the relevant authorities before making
personal arrangements.

*We have attempted to acknowledge all known sources. We apologise for any that have
been missed. Please contact us so that we can include an acknowledgement in the next
edition.*

Contents

Preface		7
Abbreviations		8

1 Maximising the State Pension — 11

Categories of state pension	12
Basic pension	13
Additional pension (SERPS) and S2P	18
Graduated pension	23
Minimum income guarantee	23
Other benefits	25

2 Joining an Occupational Scheme — 28

Types of scheme	30
Questions to ask before joining	32
Inland Revenue limits	33
Additional voluntary contributions	34
Leaving the scheme	37
Retirement	41
Death benefits	44

3 Starting a Personal Pension — 49

Contributions	51
Questions to ask before joining	54
Changing jobs	55
Retirement	55
Group personal pensions (GPPs)	56
Stakeholder pensions	57
Individual pension accounts	59

4 Understanding Annuities — 62

Types of annuity	63
Annuity rates	66
Income drawdown	69

	Phased retirement	*73*
	Voluntary purchase	*74*

5   Other Pension Formats   76

Executive pension plans (EPPs) — *78*
Small self-administered schemes (SSASs) — *79*
Self-invested personal pensions (SIPPs) — *81*
Funded unapproved retirement benefit schemes (FURBSs) — *83*
Pension mortgages — *85*
Pensions and divorce — *86*

6   Retirement Planning   89

Other savings — *90*
Getting pension forecasts — *95*
Assessing your post-retirement position — *95*
Supplementing your income — *96*
Retiring early — *98*
Late retirement — *101*

Appendices

A *Pension regulatory bodies* — *104*
B *Contribution conditions for the state basic pension* — *107*
C *Calculating the additional pension* — *111*
D *Early retirement: inflation increases in the additional pension* — *112*

Preface

It is never too early or too late to start paying into a pension scheme. Many pensions turn out to be less than expected.

With current tax relief, for those on a marginal tax rate of 22%, a pension contribution of £100 costs only £78 (and for those on 40% only £60) and then earns income free of income and capital gains tax (except that tax deducted from dividends cannot be recovered). So pensions are a very tax-efficient investment.

Income tax is, of course, deducted from pensions in the course of payment, but a substantial tax-free lump sum can often be taken on retirement.

A useful rough guide is that, to achieve a pension of £20,000 a year starting from 65, a man needs to pay about £250 a month if starting at age 30, £500 starting at 40 and £1,000 at 50. Women should add 10%.

So it pays to start as early as possible as funds are building up on a tax-free basis.

John Claxton

Abbreviations

APP	appropriate (approved) personal pension
AVCs	additional voluntary contributions
CARE	career-average revalued earnings
COD	contracted-out deduction
COMBS	company occupational mixed-benefit scheme
CPA	compulsory purchase annuity
DWP	Department of Work and Pensions
EPP	executive pension plan
ERF	early-retirement factor
FOS	Financial Ombudsman Service
FPS	final pensionable salary
FSAVCs	free-standing AVCs
GMP	guaranteed minimum pension
GPP	group personal pension
HRP	home responsibility protection
IFA	independent finanacial adviser
IPA	individual pension account
ISA	individual savings account
LEL	lower earnings limit
LPI	limited price inflation
NAEs	national average earnings
NAP	notional additional pension
NICs	National Insurance contributions
OPAS	Occupational Pensions Advisory Service
OPRA	Occupational Pensions Regulatory Authority
PA	pensionable age
PEP	personal equity plan
PLA	purchased life annuity
RPI	retail price index
SERPS	state earnings-related pension scheme
SIPP	self-invested personal pension
SPA	state pension age
SSAS	small self-administered scheme
S2P	state second pension
TESSA	tax-efficient special savings account
UEL	upper earnings limit

*To the memory of
my mother and father*

Chapter 1

Maximising the State Pension

In this chapter:

- **categories of state pension**
- **basic pension**
- **additional pension (SERPS) and S2P**
- **graduated pension**
- **minimum income guarantee**
- **other benefits.**

All state pensions are taxable and amounts are adjusted annually in line with inflation.

There are four categories of state pension, the main one being category A, which is based on your own National Insurance contributions (NICs). The state basic pension is currently about 17% of national average earnings (NAEs) and, as it is adjusted in line with inflation rather than NAEs (which normally grow at a faster rate), it is eroding over time as a percentage. Some say that, by the year 2020, it will have fallen to only 10% of NAEs.

There is a campaign to restore the relationship with NAEs but, in any case, the basic pension is not enough on its own. Hence the recent introduction of a minimum income guarantee for pensioners.

From April 2002 the current additional pension (SERPS) has been replaced by a new second state pension (SSP).

> **Is this you?**
> - I have never made National Insurance contributions. Do I get a state pension?
> - My state basic pension will not be the full amount because I have missed contributions. Can I make them up?
> - I am contracted out of SERPS – what does that mean?
> - Someone I know gets a graduated pension. Will I?
> - Are there any limitations to the minimum income guarantee?
> - I have been receiving incapacity benefit. What will happen when I reach state retirement age?

Categories of state pension

The four categories of state pension are as follows:

- **A** This is the main category and it includes both the basic pension and the additional pension. It is based on National Insurance contributions (NICs) made by yourself.

> The main category, A, is based on your own National Insurance contributions.

♦ **B** This is also based on NICs, but not your own. It is payable because of your spouse's contributions. It includes both the basic and additional pensions. The category B pension for those who are not widowed is limited to married women but will be extended to married men in April 2010.
♦ **C** A category C pension is not contributory and applies solely to the basic pension. Only those who reached pensionable age by 5 July 1948 are eligible, so further claims are unlikely.
♦ **D** Also non-contributory, this is payable when you reach 80. It only applies to the basic pension.

Basic pension

The state retirement age is currently 60 for women, 65 for men, but the age for women is being progressively increased to 65. For a woman born after 5 April 1950, a month is added to the retirement age for each month (or part) that her date of birth was after 5 April 1950. A full table is shown in the Department for Work and Pensions (DWP) *Guide to Retirement Pensions* (reference no. NP46). All women born after 5 April 1955 will retire at 65.

The amount of basic pension you receive depends on sufficient contributions having been made. When nearing retirement age, and especially if retiring early, you should check your contribution position as additional contributions can be made to catch up on any shortfall. Ask your local DWP Office for an application form for a retirement pension forecast (form BR 19), which you are entitled to at any time up to four months before you reach retirement age.

> At least four months before you reach retirement age, get a pension forecast.

Just before retirement age you should receive from the DWP Office a statement showing your total state pension entitlement (including any SERPS – see below – and graduated pension you are entitled to). After retirement you receive a statement each year showing the increased amount payable following the annual increase.

A single contributor currently receives a pension of £75.50 a week if full contributions have been made. This amount will continue to be increased in line with price inflation, not earnings, but the increase in April 2003 will be to at least £100 a year and future increases will always be at least 2.5%. Your basic pension is automatically increased when you reach the age of 80 – currently by a magnificent 25p a week!

The DWP Office calculates your entitlement but if you wish to check it you need to work through the rather complicated contribution conditions set out in Appendix B.

> You cannot get any basic pension unless you meet the contribution conditions.

Home responsibility protection (HRP)
This helps to protect the basic pension contribution qualification for those who have not been able to have regular employment because they have been caring for children or for a sick or disabled person at home. It applies since April 1978. The number of years for which you get HRP is taken away from the number of qualifying years otherwise needed to calculate your basic pension.

HRP must be applied for unless you have been in receipt of child benefit, when it will be automatically be given to you.

> Check whether you are entitled to home responsibility protection.

Christmas bonus
This bonus is paid with your December pension payment. At present it is £10. If your spouse has also reached state pension age, a second payment of £10 will be made.

Deferring receipt of the pension
The pension will be increased if you decide to postpone claiming it, up to age 70 for men, 65 for

women (at present). The increment is about 7.5% a year, not a very good deal as it takes some 12 years to recover the amount sacrificed.

> From April 2010, the increment (if you defer claiming your pension) will be increased from 7.5% to about 10.4% a year and the age limit will be removed.

You can gain the same level of increase if you give up your pension after you have started receiving it but you can only do this once and you must be below 70 (men) 65 (women). After April 2010 this age limit will also be removed.

If you are a married man you must have your wife's consent to deferring the pension, if hers is a category B pension based yours (see below), because she will have to give up hers, too. From April 2010 this need for consent will also apply to married women.

You lose the Christmas bonus if you are not receiving the pension.

You can get your pension back at any time (up to the age of 70 for men, 65 (at present) for women prior to April 2010).

Category B pensions
Most people are aware that, when both husband and wife have reached state retirement age (at present 65 and 60, respectively), if the wife is not entitled to the

state basic pension in her own right, she can apply for one based on her husband's contributions.

The amount she gets is 60% of the pension received by her husband. This is currently £45.20 a week and will increase in April 2003 to at least £60 a week.

If a wife's entitlement to a pension is less than 60% of her husband's rate, she can apply for an increase to that level.

These are examples of category B pensions, but there are others that are less well known, such as the following:

- If a husband reaches retirement age and starts receiving his pension but his wife is below retirement age, he may be able to get an increased pension for his wife, which would be paid until she reaches 60.
- All these rights apply to a wife even if she is not living with her husband.
- They will be extended to husbands from 6 April 2010.
- When a widow reaches retirement age, or subsequently becomes widowed, and her pension is less than was her husband's, she can apply for a pension equal to his, i.e. up from 60% to 100%. This right extends to widowers but in both cases is lost on re-marriage. (There are said to be many widows who are not aware of this right.)
- A divorced wife or husband whose pension is less

than that of the former spouse can apply for an equal pension, if both have reached retirement age.

Category B pensions have to be applied for, on form BRI, which is available from the DWP Office.

> If you are entitled to a category B pension, you must apply for it.

Further information on category B pensions is given in the *Guide to Retirement Pensions* booklet.

Category D pensions

These are the same as the basic category B pension (currently £45.20 a week) and are available if you reach the age of 80 and are not entitled to any other state basic pension or the one you are entitled to is less. There is a residential qualifying period.

Additional pension (SERPS) and S2P

This was formerly called the state earnings-related pension scheme and is still known as SERPS.

Subject to contracting out (see below), the additional pension is paid in respect of each year you have made NICs in respect of earnings as an employee between the lower and upper earnings limits – currently £88.75 and £585 a week. It is not available to the self-employed.

> You are entitled to the additional pension if you have paid NICs and are not contracted out.

Calculating the additional pension is complicated. The formula changed with effect from April 2000 and will result in gradually lower amounts over the next few years. Details of the calculation are given in the *Guide to Retirement Pensions* booklet, and in Appendix C.

Like the basic pension, the additional pension is adjusted annually for inflation after payment starts.

Contracting out

Many occupational schemes contract all members out of the additional pension. The scheme must guarantee a pension of no less than would have been received. It must also provide for a pension for a surviving spouse.

In the case of occupational defined benefit schemes, this was called the guaranteed minimum pension (GMP) up to 1997. Since April 1997 schemes have been required to offer pensions at 65 that are 'broadly equivalent' at least, to a specified reference scheme and GMPs no longer accrue.

> Contracted-out pension schemes must guarantee a pension at the level of additional pension that would otherwise be received.

Lower NICs are paid by the employee in respect of contracted-out pensions, the difference being called a rebate (the current rebate being 1.6%).

Employees who have a personal pension can also contract out if their scheme is an appropriate personal pension (APP). Instead of an employee contribution rebate, the scheme receives a payment based on NICs, which must be claimed by the pension provider.

Personal pensions and occupational defined contribution pensions that are contracted out must provide a protected rights fund in place of the additional pension. Benefits accruing after 6 April 1997 are subject to the statutory rule for limited price inflation (LPI) – i.e. retail price inflation up to 5% per annum in respect of benefits earned after 6 April 1997.

Post-retirement increases in the GMP

These are met in full by the state in respect of the amount earned by contributions up to 1988. Thereafter the scheme is required to pay the increases up to 3% a year; if annual inflation is higher, the state pays the excess over 3%.

> If you are entitled to a GMP, part of the post-retirement increase will come from the state and part from your employer.

This already complicated position can worsen in the case of early retirement because the GMP does not come into play until the state pension age (SPA) is reached.

Since GMPs were discontinued in 1997, post-retirement increases will gradually reduce in importance but will take many years to disappear entirely. Details are given in the *Guide to Retirement Pensions* booklet and in Appendix D.

Widowed spouses

Category B pensions (see above) extend to the additional pension, so a widowed spouse is entitled to receive an additional pension based on the deceased spouse's contributions. This was to be cut by 50% for those widowed after 5 April 2000, but now the cut only applies to men and women reaching state pension age (65/60) after 5 October 2002.

Furthermore, the cut will be phased in over 10 years from October 2002, so only those reaching state pension age after 5 October 2010 will be fully affected. Those who reach it between 2002 and 2004 will receive 90%, between 2004 and 2006 80%, between 2006 and 2008 70%, and 2008 and 2010 60%.

> The reduction in category B additional pensions for widows from 100% to 50% will be phased in from 2002 to 2010.

The new state second pension (S2P)

This replaced SERPS in April 2002 in respect of future earnings (accrued SERPS up to 2 April 2002 are kept). It is earnings-related and applies to all earnings above £3,900 a year.

The main advantage of the change is for those earning between £3,900 and £10,800, because their S2P will be calculated as if their earnings were £10,800. That amount will be adjusted in later years in line with earnings rather than prices.

The S2P for those with earnings above £10,800 will be at least as much as under SERPS. Contracting out still applies.

Also, unlike SERPS, S2P is extended to certain people who cannot work, such as carers and the sick or disabled. However it has not been extended to the self-employed.

S2P may become a flat rate pension from the year 2006. The effect for high earners could be a lower future pension accrual than under SERPS, although anyone who has then reached a certain age (believed to be 45) will continue under the earnings-related S2P and so will still receive at least as much as under SERPS.

> SERPS was replaced by the new state second pension (S2P) from April 2002.

Graduated pension

Before SERPS was introduced in 1975 there was another state second pension, called the graduated pension, which operated from 1961. There was no contracting out.

The amount received depends on the number of units of graduated contributions you paid over the period and the value of a unit at the time you claim your pension.

To work out the number of units, add together all your graduated contributions and divide by 7.5 for men, 9 for women (the different calculation for women will cease in the year 2010). The value of a unit is shown in the DWP Office leaflet GL23. As an example, in 1995 it was 7.64p.

Your pension forecast and annual statement referred to under the basic pension will also include any amounts for the graduated pension.

Minimum income guarantee

Pensioners on small incomes can now receive the benefit of the minimum income guarantee, which is calculated at about 20% of average earnings. Single pensioners are currently guaranteed a minimum income of £100 a week (£154 for a married couple), with higher amounts for those aged over 75, and higher still if over 80. The amounts are to be adjusted annually in line with earnings rather than price inflation.

The extra income over the state basic pension is paid as income support, so recipients must be eligible for that. Other income is set off against the extra amount. Income from savings is not taken into account but, if your savings exceed £6,000, £1 a week for every £250 of savings above £6,000 is added to your income, reducing the extra to nil when savings reach £12,000, even without any other income.

> You must be entitled to income support to get the minimum income guarantee.

The minimum income guarantee will be replaced in April 2003 by a new pensions credit, which will benefit pensioners who currently lose out on the guarantee because they have other pensions and/or modest savings.

A guarantee credit will remain as a minimum income above the state basic pension.

A savings credit will be added to the basic pension at a rate of 60p for every £1 of other income, which will include other pensions and savings beyond £6,000. Savings will be valued as income at 10% of the capital value.

The excess of other income over the guarantee will be cut back at the rate of 40p for every £1. The maximum savings credit over the guarantee is estimated to be £13.80 a week in 2003 (£18.60 for a married couple).

Other benefits

There are complicated rules if you are receiving any of the following benefits when you reach retirement age:

- incapacity benefit
- reduced-earnings allowance
- severe disablement allowance
- invalid care allowance.

The effects are different in each case and you need to find out what they are in respect of any benefit you are receiving. Details are given in the *Guide to Retirement Pensions* booklet. What you find could cause you to decide to defer drawing the state pension.

Normally, if you are receiving any other benefit, your basic pension will be reduced on a pound-for-pound basis. However, any additional pension or graduated pension will not be affected.

> Your basic pension may be reduced if you are receiving other benefits.

But you can get the basic pension as well as

- attendance allowance
- disability living allowance.

You should also remember that, when you start to receive your pension, a benefit received by someone as your dependant may be reduced, so you may wish to take that into account.

Winter fuel payment

All pensioner households (that is, where at least one person is over state retirement age) receive currently £150 winter fuel payment.

Free TV licence

Anyone over the age of 75 gets a free TV licence.

Action points

- **Do you know your state basic pension position, especially if you are nearing retirement? If not, get a pensions forecast. If your contributions are inadequate, consider paying in more to achieve the full pension.**

- **Work out whether you or your spouse will be entitled to a category B pension.**

- **If you are not contracted out, watch for the effect on you of the introduction of the new state second pension in 2002.**

- **If you were working before 1975, make sure you get the graduated pension. When you retire, check on the unit value.**

- **If your retirement income is below the guaranteed minimum, make sure you get the extra to bring you up to the guaranteed amount, subject to a cutback if your assets exceed £6,000. If they do, watch for the introduction of the proposed pension credit in 2003, because you might then qualify for more.**

- **If you are the recipient of other state benefits, such as incapacity benefit, you should find out what will be the impact on them when you start to receive the state pension.**

Chapter 2

Joining an Occupational Scheme

In this chapter:

- **types of scheme**
- **questions to ask before joining**
- **Inland Revenue limits**
- **additional voluntary contributions**
- **leaving the scheme**
- **retirement**
- **death benefits.**

Occupational schemes are arranged by an employer for employees. They are governed by a trust deed and rules.

There are two basic types of occupational schemes – final salary and money purchase. A number of pertinent questions should be asked before joining your employer's scheme. All approved pension schemes are subject to Inland Revenue limits to contributions and benefits. All schemes are required to have a facility for additional voluntary contributions (AVCs), and anyone who can afford it and is not up to the Inland Revenue limits should consider doing so, subject to giving first consideration to the new stakeholder pension.

The scheme rules will spell out exactly what happens if you leave the company's employment and if you decide to leave the pension scheme whilst still an employee.

There will also be rules about retirement (whether it takes place on normal retirement date, earlier or later) and about death benefits. If your employer has a scheme you should consider joining it before deciding to take out a personal pension, because otherwise you may lose the advantage of the employer's contribution.

Is this you?
- I have been paying for a personal pension but my new employer has a company scheme. Should I join?
- What do I need to know about the scheme before joining?
- I would like to pay in more but I am told my contribution would exceed the Inland Revenue limits – what are they?
- What are AVCs?
- I have been made redundant. What happens to my pension?
- I would like to retire early. Would I still get the full pension?
- What happens to my pension if I die?

Types of scheme

There are two basic types of occupational pension schemes.

Final salary

Also called defined benefit, this is the best form of pension for an employee because the benefits are fixed and so the pension amount is known in advance to some degree of certainty.

> Final salary schemes are the best type for employees, as there is more certainty about the pension amount.

The contributions vary but, in practice, the employee contribution is normally a fixed percentage of salary and the employer pays the rest. Some schemes are non-contributory for the employee.

The pension is based on the final pensionable salary (FPS), i.e. that received immediately before retirement, or a formula such as the average of the last 3 years, or even the best 3 consecutive years in the last 10.

The amount of pension is calculated by multiplying the FPS by a fraction in respect of each year of service, such as 1/60, which achieves a 50% pension after 30 year's service (called a 60ths scheme).

Final salary schemes are usually contracted out of the state additional pension scheme.

> Final salary schemes are usually contracted out.

Career-average revalued earnings (CARE) schemes
This is a more sophisticated kind of defined benefit scheme, but it is not often seen. The difference is that, instead of a final salary, the basis of the pension is the total of each year's earnings revalued in line with an index such as the retail price index (RPI), divided by the number of years.

Some pension experts favour this method because it has the advantage over normal final salary schemes of being unaffected by volatile earnings and the inclusion of part-timers, and leavers get the same benefits as stayers. These are among the advantages of money purchase schemes but the member still has known benefits.

Money purchase
Also called defined contribution, money purchase scheme contributions are fixed and the benefit varies, which is much less attractive to the employee but much more to the employer (many employers have switched new employees to money purchase). Most of the accumulated funds must eventually be used to buy an annuity.

The disadvantage to the employee is twofold: not knowing in advance how much the invested contributions will earn and also what pension the final amount will purchase.

> For employees, money purchase schemes are not as good as final salary schemes – because of uncertainty.

Sometimes the two types are combined in one scheme offering mixed benefits. These are called COMBS (company occupational mixed-benefit schemes). The mixture may be final salary up to a specified salary level and money purchase thereafter.

Questions to ask before joining

It is nearly always advantageous to join a company scheme but, first, you should get more information about the scheme.

> Get full information about your company scheme before deciding whether to join.

Ask the following questions:

- Is it final salary or money purchase?
- Is it contracted out of the state additional pension scheme?
- What are the contribution rates – employer and employee?
- Can a tax-free lump sum be taken on retirement?
- Is there a contingent spouse's pension?
- What happens in the event of death, in service and in retirement, and is any lump sum payable kept out of your estate?

- What happens if employment is ended, by either party?
- What would be the effect of being laid off without pay, or short-time working?

And if it is a final salary scheme:

- How is the pension calculated?
- Is there any post-retirement adjustment for inflation above the statutory limited price indexation, and is it guaranteed or discretionary?

> Limited price indexation (LPI) is full indexation up to 5% per annum, calculated on the retail price index in respect of benefits earned after 6 April 1997.

- What are the rules for early and late retirement and is there any difference if early retirement is due to ill-health?

Armed with the answers to these questions, you can decide whether to join your employer's scheme.

Inland Revenue limits

Contributions to an approved scheme and income earned (except dividends) are tax free if certain limits are not exceeded (company rules may impose lower amounts).

The Inland Revenue limits are as follows:

- *Maximum pensionable salary* – for joiners since 14 March 1989, £97,200 (this is reviewed annually in the budget). No limit for earlier joiners.
- *Maximum pension* – two thirds of FPS (which can include fringe benefits).
- *Maximum for spouse on death of pensioner* – two thirds of the pensioner's maximum (i.e. four ninths of FPS).
- *Minimum service for maximum pension* – 20 years (i.e. thirtieths) for joiners since 17 March 1987, 10 years if earlier.
- *Contribution limit for employee* – 15% of salary (none for employer).
- *Post-retirement adjustment* – full inflation.
- *Lump sum cash* – 2.25 times initial pension for joiners since 1 June 1988, 1.5 times FPS after 20 years' service (reduced in proportion if less service) for earlier joiners.

> Be aware of the Inland Revenue limits – hardly anyone reaches them all.

Additional voluntary contributions

All occupational schemes are now required to have arrangements for members to make additional voluntary contributions (AVCs), and anyone who can afford it and is not up to Inland Revenue limits should certainly consider doing so.

The maximum employee contribution to the main scheme and AVCs together is 15% of pay. As the usual level of employee contribution to the main scheme is 5%, there is ample scope for AVCs and, of course, if there is no employee contribution at all to the main scheme the full 15% is available.

> Check whether there is scope for you to make AVCs, within the Inland Revenue 15% employee contribution limit.

Additional benefits earned in an AVC are usually on a money-purchase basis but may be in the form of additional years of service, which should be better.

Free-standing AVCs (FSAVCs) are outside the company scheme. Whilst giving more freedom, they are probably more expensive as you must pay the administrative costs instead of the company.

AVC benefits can be taken at any time between the ages of 50 and 75 (as with personal pensions), if the scheme permits, irrespective of whether you have retired from the main scheme. For AVCs commencing after 8 April 1987, it is not possible to take part as a lump sum. For this reason it is worth considering a stakeholder pension (see Chapter 3) instead of some or all of your future AVCs, as it will then be possible to take the tax-free lump sum.

> The new stakeholder pension may be a better alternative than AVCs.

ISAs versus AVCs and stakeholder pensions

There has been some debate about whether AVCs are better value than individual savings accounts (ISAs), and this now extends to stakeholder pensions. With AVCs and stakeholder pensions, the contributions are tax free but the benefits are taxable. With ISAs it is the opposite. All are free of income and capital gains taxes (except for income tax on dividends) whilst the money is in the scheme. Charges might be higher for AVCs than for ISAs but stakeholder charges may be lower.

Most experts favour AVCs/stakeholder pensions because the tax relief comes at the beginning, so funds accumulate on a tax-free basis. ISAs have more freedom of action, but is this a good thing for pension money? The comparison is further confused by the discontinuation of tax credits for dividend income in pension schemes from 1997 and in ISAs from 2004.

You can, of course, invest in AVCs, stakeholders and ISAs, if you can afford it.

> If your funds are limited, weigh up carefully the relative merits of AVCs, stakeholder pensions and ISAs.

Also worth bearing in mind is the freedom to make transfers from ISAs to stakeholder pensions (see Chapter 3).

Leaving the scheme

There can be a number of reasons for leaving the scheme but it usually arises because of leaving the company's employment. Only those with less than two years' membership of the scheme can obtain a refund of contributions on leaving and 20% is deducted for tax. Otherwise it is a question of leaving behind a preserved pension (a pension payable from some date in the future, usually the normal retirement date for the scheme – often called a deferred pension) or taking a transfer to another scheme, including a personal pension scheme.

> If you change jobs, you need to decide whether to take your pension with you or leave it behind.

Preserved pension

It is now a requirement for all preserved pensions earned after April 1997 to be increased in line with inflation up to 5% a year, until normal retirement date. Few schemes do more than this, although there is nothing to prevent them from going beyond the 5% limit if inflation is higher.

Transfers

The first thing to remember is that there is no hurry because a transfer can be taken at any time. The way transfers work is that the actuary of the existing scheme calculates a transfer value, this being the capital value of the accrued benefits. You should then ask the new scheme what benefits the transfer value will buy.

An occupational scheme may offer additional years' service for a transfer in, but usually it will be a fixed amount of pension, which is a poorer alternative because there is no protection against future inflation.

When comparing, it is important to take account of all the benefits in the existing scheme, including any subsequent inflation proofing.

> When deciding whether or not to transfer, you need to take all the benefits into account.

The following points should be borne in mind when considering a transfer:

- The employer usually pays the administrative costs of a company scheme, whereas the member pays in a personal scheme.
- Final salary is more certain than money purchase (personal pensions are invariably money purchase).
- A company scheme may make discretionary increases to pensions, over and above the statutory increases.

Persons who took a transfer to a personal pension when leaving between April 1988 and June 1994 may have been given bad advice and are included in a review currently being undertaken. Compensation may be available.

All those who were sold a personal pension between 1988 and 1994 should have received a questionnaire from their pension provider. Fee-paid help and free legal advice is available. The Financial Services Authority have urged occupational schemes to take members back.

> If you were wrongly advised to take a transfer to a personal pension between April 1988 and June 1994, you may be entitled to compensation.

Opt-outs

This term is used to describe decisions by existing employees to leave the company scheme in favour of a personal pension, even though they are not leaving their employment. (New employees who decide not to join their employer's scheme are called non-joiners.)

The first opt-outs commenced in February 1981 and they are called section 32 buy-outs (after the relevant section of the Act). In many ways these mirror the company scheme, using the same retirement ages and tax-free cash rules and the same requirements for GMPs (see Chapter 1) if they were contracted out. They can now be transferred to personal pensions, which will overcome the retirement age restriction. Opt-outs from company schemes to personal pensions were permitted from July 1988.

The same questions arise for opt-outs and non-joiners as for transfers (see above), including possible bad advice between 1988 and 1994.

> Opting out or not joining your employers scheme needs the same careful consideration as taking a transfer.

Sensible switching to a personal pension

Whilst opting out or not joining is generally a bad decision, since the employer's contribution is lost, it can make sense for some people to switch to a personal pension shortly before retiring.

Most occupational schemes make provision for spouses' pensions. If you are single, find out the transfer value of your accrued pension (which will include an amount for the contingent spouse pension) and check whether you can buy an annuity that gives you a better return. Be sure you are comparing like with like so that, for example, the annuity carries the same inflation-proofing as the occupational pension. Spouses' pensions may only apply if you are married so, if you have a partner but are not married, the same argument applies.

Another potential area is if you are in poor health at the time of retirement. Again, occupational schemes makes no allowance for a possible premature death, whereas in those circumstances you might be able to buy an impaired life annuity that pays out more than an ordinary one (see Chapter 4 for annuities).

> If your scheme provides a widowed spouse pension
> and you are not married, or if you are in poor
> health, it might pay to take a transfer to a personal
> pension immediately before retiring.

A point to bear in mind is that the tax-free cash on retirement in respect of a transfer/opt-out from an occupational scheme to a personal pension is 25% of the fund derived from the transfer value. However, if you are a controlling director or you earn in excess of the earnings cap and are over the age of 44, the cash is limited to the lesser of 25% and the amount you could have received from the company scheme (called the certified amount).

Retirement

Most people retire on their pension scheme normal retirement date but early retirement has become increasingly popular. On the other hand, some people are tempted to keep on working and to take late retirement.

Normal retirement

Traditionally, normal retirement date is the same as for the state scheme, although sometimes a company has a scheme in which normal retirement is earlier, perhaps at 62. As you approach normal retirement date the scheme will provide a statement showing your pension entitlement and the effects of choosing to take cash, if this is permitted (it usually is).

> Your pension scheme will provide a statement of your pension entitlement shortly before normal retirement date.

Final salary occupational pensions commence on retirement whether normal, early or late, but money-purchase schemes can now offer the right to defer purchasing an annuity up till age 75, with income drawdown in the mean time (as with personal pensions).

Early retirement

Early retirement pensions are lower for two reasons: less service and earlier payment. In the case of final salary schemes, the latter is dealt with by the application of an early-retirement factor (ERF) to the pension, usually at least 4% for each year not worked.

> If you are planning to retire early, find out how much your pension will reduce.

Many schemes waive the ERF in the case of ill-health early retirement, and employers wishing to encourage early retirement may eliminate it by paying in extra (see Chapter 6 for more information on early retirement).

Late retirement

Final salary schemes normally provide some advantage for delaying retirement – to compensate for the pension not drawn. Of course, the employer has to agree to the deferred retirement. The alternative is to take the pension and then return to work. Which to choose depends on the figures, taking account of the income tax implications.

> You cannot defer your retirement date unless your employer agrees.

(Chapter 6 also gives more information on late retirement.)

Cash lump sum on retirement

Most schemes have an option to take a tax-free lump sum on retirement. It is pleasant to have this decision to make, but it may not be easy. Remember you can choose to take as much cash as you like, free of tax, up to the scheme limit, but you lose pension in proportion.

The pension statement you receive shortly before retirement will show how much cash you can take and the effect on your pension.

If the pension is fully inflation-proofed, it might be better to leave the money in. Otherwise, check whether you can buy an annuity with the cash to provide a higher income after tax than the pension forgone.

If you wish to pay off your mortgage, or at least reduce it, it could be worth taking some cash out (again it is possible to calculate and compare the alternatives). But think carefully before you take the cash to buy a new car or a special holiday!

Post-retirement adjustments

All final salary schemes must adjust pensions in payment that have been earned during the period since 1997, by the rate of price inflation up to 5%. This is called limited price indexation (LPI).

Some schemes contract to do better, such as adjustment of pensions earned up to 1997. Some provide for full inflation. Others may make discretionary increases if inflation exceeds the 5% level.

> Find out whether your pension scheme pays higher increases than the statutory minimum.

Death benefits

Death in service

Many occupational schemes include a death benefit payable to your dependants in the event of death in service. It is usually a multiple of annual pay at the time of death (commonly three times).

Most schemes provide a nomination form when you join for you to nominate whom you wish to receive the death benefit if you die. The trustees are not bound to follow your direction but they usually do. The advantage of completing the nomination form is that the benefit then falls outside your estate for inheritance tax purposes and does not have to await probate (or letters of administration if you have not made a will) before being paid out.

> Have you nominated whom you wish to receive the death benefit if you die in service?

Instead of a lump sum, some pension schemes provide a pension for your survivors – your spouse and dependent children – usually calculated on your accrued pension at the date of your death, perhaps one half for your spouse and one quarter for each dependent child up to a maximum of three children. The children's pension will cease when they are no longer dependent (perhaps at age 18 or after ceasing full-time education).

Some people consider a lump sum is better than a pension in these circumstances, in case there is a mortgage to pay off, but most people have life assurance to cover mortgage repayment. Also, there is a danger a lump sum may not be used sensibly to provide a future income.

Death in retirement

Usually there is no death benefit once you have retired but many schemes provide a contingent spouse's pension, so-called because it is contingent upon your death before your spouse.

> Does your scheme provide a spouse's pension if you die first?

The rate is commonly half the rate paid to the pensioner (the Inland Revenue limit is two thirds). There may, in addition, be pensions payable to any dependent children, possibly half the spouse's pension for each one up to a maximum of three.

The best schemes base the contingent spouse's pension on the amount of the member's pension before taking tax-free cash and also index it at the same rate as they use for pensions in payment. Some schemes guarantee the payment of the first few years' pension (commonly 5 years) in addition to the spouse's pension. If you die within that period an additional amount equal to the balance of pension not yet paid goes to your dependants.

> Check whether your scheme has a guaranteed minimum period for pension payment.

Death when a deferred pensioner
You are a deferred pensioner if you leave behind a deferred pension when your employment ceased. Usually in this case the scheme rules do not provide a death benefit; instead, a spouse's pension is paid, probably of one half the deferred pension including any post-leaving increases, possibly plus something for dependent children.

Make sure you know and understand what the pension scheme rules say about death benefits and either explain it to your beneficiaries or leave a note with your will (you have made a will, haven't you?).

> Do your beneficiaries know what to expect from the pension scheme when you die?

Action points

- **If you are a member of an occupational pension scheme, do you know whether it is a final salary or money purchase scheme, and are you aware of the implications for you?**

- **If you are contemplating joining your employer's scheme, have you asked all the right questions?**

- **Do you know how the Inland Revenue limits apply to your scheme?**

- **Have you considered making AVCs and/or starting a stakeholder pension, to supplement your company pension?**

- **If you are thinking about leaving your occupational scheme (or not joining if you are a new employee), are you fully aware of what you are giving up?**

- **Have you considered the financial implications of retirement, whether early, at normal retirement age or late, including whether to take any cash lump sum available?**

- **If your pension scheme includes a lump sum death benefit, make sure you have completed a nomination form so the trustees know your wishes and the benefit is paid outside your estate.**

Chapter 3

Starting a Personal Pension

In this chapter:

- **contributions**
- **questions to ask before joining**
- **changing jobs**
- **retirement**
- **group personal pensions (GPPs)**
- **stakeholder pensions**
- **individual pension accounts.**

> Personal pensions are suitable for people who cannot (or do not wish to) join a company scheme, the self-employed, those who change jobs frequently and those in irregular work.

The basis of personal pensions is money purchase, so there is no guarantee of the benefit amount. Most schemes are either unit linked or on a with-profits basis. Unit linked have the disadvantage of being tied to some extent to the stock market, which might be low when you retire, although there are now ways round this. With-profits schemes have the advantage that bonuses, once declared, are guaranteed. However, they are less flexible and so investment performance may suffer. Unitised with-profits schemes are a combination in that they are invested in units but bonuses are secure.

Unit linked personal pension schemes may be invested in units in a pension fund or directly in a unit or investment trust.

> **Is this you?**
> - I am self-employed and haven't bothered about pensions until now. Should I start a personal pension? How much can I pay in?
> - What do I need to know about a scheme before joining?
> - I am changing my job – what happens about my personal pension?
> - When can I start to draw my personal pension?
> - What is a group personal pension?
> - I have no earned income and have been told I cannot pay into a pension scheme. Is that correct?
> - What are the advantages of an individual pension account?

Contributions

These are usually paid regularly each month but can be irregular, and some people prefer to wait until the year end to see how much they can afford. A regular payment has a certain discipline but you may be tied to a contract and charges tend to be higher. With lump sum payments you can shop around each time. Either way, a flexible arrangement is sensible so you can increase, reduce or even stop contributions at will. You can also combine the two by making a regular contribution and topping it up at the year end.

> You can make regular contributions, or wait till the year end, or combine the two.

There is an advantage to regular payments into a pension invested in equities. It is called pound-cost averaging, a curious description of the fact that, when the stock market is low, you get more shares or units for your money than when it is high, so that the average price per share/unit is less than the average of the prices paid each time you invest.

It is sensible to start a personal pension at an early age, even with a relatively small payment, because you can always increase the amount in the future.

If you have a concern about not being able to keep up your contributions should you become too ill to work, you can arrange for insurance, possibly through your chosen pension provider.

Inland Revenue limits

Maximum contributions are a percentage of earnings, related to age at the beginning of the current tax year, as follows:

	%
35 or less	17.5
36–45	20
46–50	25
51–55	30
56–60	35
61 and over	40

> Earnings-related contribution limits increase with age.

These amounts are subject to the same earnings limit as occupational schemes (i.e. currently £97,200). Contributions can also be made by 31 January in any year in respect of the previous tax year if you did not contribute the maximum then. Tax relief applies at the income tax rates then in force.

Now that stakeholder pensions are available (see below), it is possible to make annual contributions of up to £3,600 (including the tax rebate) to personal or stakeholder pensions, or both together – the earnings-related limits only applying to higher levels of contributions.

> The earnings-related limits only apply to contributions above £3,600 a year.

If life cover is included, the cost of it counts towards the contribution limits.

You can continue to make contributions to a personal pension for up to 5 years after retirement (if you can afford to), based on your final year's earnings.

Retirement annuity plans
These were discontinued for new people after 30 June 1988 in favour of personal pensions, but existing plans on that date continue. There is no earnings cap in this case but maximum contribution rates are lower, as follows:

	%
50 or less	17.5
51–55	20
56–60	22.5
61 and over	27.5

Contracting out
Personal pensions can be contracted out in the same way as occupational schemes. They are then called appropriate personal pensions (APPs). There is no rebate; instead, the Department of Social Security make equivalent payments to the APP, which initially have to be requested by the pension provider.

> Personal pensions can be contracted-out of the state additional pension.

Questions to ask before joining

Shop around with a list of questions:

- How flexible can the contributions be?
- What are the charges?
- What are the penalties (if any) for stopping and transferring?
- What happens if you die before buying an annuity – is your fund protected from inheritance tax?
- Are there penalties if you decide to buy your annuity elsewhere?
- What is the past growth record of the fund you will be investing in?
- How safe will your fund be?

> Prepare a list of questions before shopping around for a personal pension.

Consider using an independent financial adviser (IFA) to help you choose a personal pension provider. Make sure they have the pension qualification. Ask about fees. Ring 0117 971 1177 for a list of IFAs in your area. A list of advisers offering fee-based advice on pensions is available from Money Management Register – ring 0117 976 9444.

Changing jobs

Personal pensions remain with you through job changes, so there is no need to consider transfers.

> Personal pensions do not have to be transferred when you change jobs.

However, if a new job carries with it an occupational scheme, it will almost certainly be worth joining. In that case the personal pension can be left as it is, without further contributions for the time being, or it can be used for making AVCs or even transferred to the company scheme if that is advantageous. (See the previous chapter for further information about the decision to transfer.)

Retirement

There is no Inland Revenue limit to the amount of the pension from a personal pension scheme. The tax-free lump sum on retirement can be up to 25% of the fund.

After taking any tax-free cash, the balance of the fund must be used to buy an annuity – but not only may the stock market be low at the critical time, but also annuity rates may be low: a double blow. However, it is now possible to defer the purchase of some or all of the annuity. This can now take place at any age between 50 and 75 and so can be postponed beyond retirement. The possible advantage of delay is that the stock market and/or annuity rates might improve.

> A personal pension must be used to buy an annuity but it can be any time between the ages 50 and 75.

If annuity purchase is deferred, income must be drawn directly from the fund within minimum and maximum percentages. The lump sum option is not affected by deferment and funds left in continue to grow free of tax. Deferment can clearly be advantageous if retirement can be phased, perhaps by working part time for a year or two. Otherwise, experts suggest it is not viable if your fund is below about £100,000.

Group personal pensions (GPPs)

Sometimes an employer without an occupational scheme will arrange for personal pensions to be available to employees through a group scheme. These are still individual personal pensions.

> Find out whether your employer has a group personal pension scheme.

The advantage may be the employer pays the administrative costs of the scheme. The employer is not obliged to make a contribution but may well do so, within the overall Inland Revenue limit.

The disadvantage is that you have no choice of pension provider, although there may be some choice of investment vehicle. Accumulated funds can be transferred from one employer to another, provided of course the new employer has a GPP – if not, you can continue as an individual personal pension. You cannot be compelled to join a group scheme; you can still arrange your own personal pension.

Stakeholder pensions

These commenced in April 2001 and employers must (subject to certain exemptions) offer their employees access to a stakeholder scheme, although employees do not have to join. Employers do not have to contribute, although they can.

> Get hold of the details of your employer's stakeholder pension scheme.

Stakeholder pensions are targeted at those earning between £10,000 and £20,000 a year (the middle earners), but can be of interest to anyone. Contributions of up to £3,600 a year can be paid even if you have no earnings. This includes the tax rebate added by the Inland Revenue to your contributions, equivalent to the standard rate of tax (i e. currently just over 22p for each 78p), so the maximum you can contribute yourself is £2,808. The tax rebate is added even if you pay no tax. Higher-rate taxpayers can claim back the 18% balance at the year end. The contribution limits above the £3,600 level are the same as for personal pensions.

There must be a payroll deduction facility for the employer's chosen scheme, but this is not compulsory if you choose to go elsewhere. The minimum individual contribution cannot be more than £20. Annual charges are capped at 1% of fund value, with no initial charges and no penalties for transferring the fund or suspending contributions. As with personal pensions, 25% can be withdrawn tax free and the balance used to buy an annuity, at any time between the ages of 50 and 75. In fact, it is possible to take this action immediately after contributing, which may appeal to you if you are already retired.

Stakeholder pensions can be held alongside existing personal pensions or company schemes (but, in the case of final salary company schemes, only if the employee earns less than £30,000 a year and is not a controlling director).

> Stakeholder pensions can be held alongside a personal pension or (with certain exceptions) a company scheme.

If you are contributing to an AVC, a stakeholder pension is worth considering as an alternative but it will be possible to have both, if you can afford it. It is possible to transfer funds from an individual savings account (ISA) to a stakeholder pension. This is an advantage if you are initially reluctant to tie up your savings in a pension but, of course, it uses up your annual ISA allowance. Another interesting use of stakeholder pensions is that they can, within the inheritance tax exemptions, be purchased for somone else – for your children or even your grandchildren (there is no minimum age).

> Consider starting stakeholder pensions for your children or grandchildren.

Individual pension accounts

If you think you have the necessary investment skills, you can put an individual pension account (IPA) wrapper around your future personal and/or stakeholder pension contributions. This enables you to choose how the money is invested and to move it around as you wish.

> You can manage your own personal pension through an individual pension account.

Investments can be in pooled pension investments (PPIs) – i.e. unit trusts and other pooled investment funds. Contributions are subject to the normal rules of personal pensions and continue to be tax deductible. Income and capital growth within the account are tax free, except for dividends. There are no additional charges. Contributions can be discontinued at any time but contributions already made must be left in the account till you are at least 50.

You need to shop around to find a provider with the widest choice of investment. Also, it is important to monitor your investments within the IPA.

> You need to monitor your investments within an individual pension account.

There is of course the risk you may not manage the investments as well as an expert.

Action points

- **Make sure you are paying the maximum personal pension contributions for your age, if you can afford to.**

- **Consider switching your personal pension if the charges are high. Get help if necessary to make the best choice of personal pension provider for you.**

- **If you change jobs, you can continue contributing to your personal pension but, if there is an occupational pension available, it will almost certainly be advantageous to join it.**

- **When you retire, you may need help in deciding whether to buy an annuity immediately or whether to wait.**

- **If your employer has a group personal pension, weigh up the pros and cons of joining.**

- **Give careful consideration to the new stakeholder pension: it could be well worth while joining, whatever your existing pension arrangements are.**

- **If you think you are a successful investor, consider putting your future contributions into an individual pension account.**

Chapter 4

Understanding Annuities

In this chapter:

- **types of annuity**
- **annuity rates**
- **income drawdown**
- **phased retirement**
- **voluntary purchase.**

An annuity provides a guaranteed income for life in return for a lump sum investment. As already explained, the funds from money purchase, personal and stakeholder pension schemes which you cannot take as tax-free cash must eventually be used to buy an annuity.

An annuity purchased from a money purchase, personal or stakeholder pension fund is called a compulsory purchase annuity (CPA) and all the receipts from it are taxable. Voluntary purchase of an annuity – such as with the tax-free lump sum, for example – is called a purchased life annuity (PLA) and only the interest element of the receipts is taxable. The provider of the annuity normally deducts tax at the savings rate (currently 20%) so, if your marginal rate is less or more, you will have to claim a refund or pay the extra.

There is a wide choice of type of annuity and also a wide variety of rates for each type, so make sure your pension provider gives you all the alternatives and makes it clear whether there is any penalty for shopping around. From September 2002 they will have to notify you of your options.

Because women on average live longer than men, their rates are lower.

The main thing to remember about annuities is that part of the receipt is capital, so normally there is nothing left when you die.

> **Is this you?**
> ♦ I have to purchase an annuity from my personal pension money but I am confused about the different types available.
> ♦ How can I find out whether the annuity rate I am being offered is a good one?
> ♦ Do I have to buy the annuity immediately I retire?
> ♦ Would it be a good idea to take my tax-free cash and buy an annuity with it?

Types of annuity

The choice of annuity is wide and you need to decide which type is best for you, a decision that will also depend on the annuity rates you can get (see the next section). In choosing between flat-rate and escalating annuities, you need to think about how long you may live, taking into account your health and your family history of life expectation – not an easy decision.

Single life

This is the basic form of annuity and it provides a flat-rate income over the life of the annuitant (the buyer of the annuity), with nothing to come at the end.

> A single-life annuity provids a flat-rate income over the life of the annuitant.

You need to remember that, even with inflation of only 3% a year, over 20 years the income will have fallen by 40% in real terms.

Joint life

In this case the flat-rate income is provided over the life of two people (usually husband and wife) and continues until the second death. It is possible to arrange a two-stage income – higher until the first death, then lower for the life of the survivor.

Indexed

Instead of a flat-rate income, it is possible to arrange for a set rate of growth in the annuity, usually 3% or 5% per annum. Clearly, the starting income is substantially lower than with a flat-rate annuity.

> An indexed annuity provides a chosen rate of annual increase.

With an escalation rate of 3%, it takes some 10 years for the payout to catch up and a further 10 years to recover the shortfall over the first 10. Bearing in mind a tendency for expenses to fall as you get older, you may prefer to take the flat-rate basis.

Impaired life

This is where the annuitant has a potentially terminal health problem, so that higher rates are available (based on the reduced life expectancy).

Investment related

In this case, instead of a fixed income, the annuity provides a variable income based on stock market performance, so it can vary both up and down (which may not suit you), although in the long run income should increase.

> An investment-related annuity provides a variable income, dependent on the performance of the underlying assets.

The annuity will be invested in a unit-linked or with-profits fund. With-profits gives a smoother performance; unit-linked (like a unit trust) is more volatile.

In the case of with-profits annuities, you usually have to choose a growth rate (called the hurdle rate) of between 0 and 5%. If your bonuses are consistently below the hurdle rate your income can fall, so it pays to choose a relatively low rate. However, it is possible to get a with-profits annuity that gives a guarantee, such as that the payout will never fall below the starting amount, though naturally at a lower starting figure.

Capital protection

Whilst annuities normally cease on the death of the annuitant, it is possible to obtain an annuity that leaves a capital sum available to the annuitant's heirs. Obviously, the capital element of the return is lower.

> You can get an annuity that leaves a capital sum payable on your death.

Annuity rates

These depend on the type of annuity, the age at which you start and the going rates of interest. In recent years, interest rates have fallen whilst life expectancy has increased – a double blow to annuity rates, which have reduced considerably.

The examples that follow are based on current rates, which can change day by day (unfortunately, usually downwards at present).

Compulsory purchase annuities

These are the annuities you eventually have to buy with most of the funds from a money purchase type pension scheme. Income tax is deductible from the whole payment.

> Income tax is deductible from the full amount of the compulsory purchase annuity you have to buy from your pension fund.

The examples of rates shown below are based on a flat-rate annuity, with a 50% spouse's benefit where applicable and are after deducting 20% income tax:

	Male %	*Female* %	*Joint* %
Single life, starting age:			
55	4.6	4.4	
60	5.1	4.8	
65	5.8	5.3	
Joint life, starting age:			
husband 60/wife 57			4.6
husband 65/wife 63			5.1

Purchased life annuities

These annuities are bought with your own money, including the tax-free cash from your pension scheme. Income tax is deductible only from the income portion of the payment, the capital repayment element being free of tax. The older you are at commencement, the higher the capital content and therefore the lower the tax payable.

> Income tax is only deductible from the income portion of the amount received from an annuity bought with your own money, called a purchased life annuity.

The rates shown below are flat rates after deducting 20% tax from the income element:

	Male %	*Female* %	*Joint* %
Single life, starting age:			
55	6.4	5.8	
60	7.2	6.4	
65	8.2	7.3	
Joint life, starting age:			
husband 60/wife 57			6.3
husband 65/wife 63			7.1

In both these examples the lower rates for females reflect their longer life expectancy. Comparing the two sets of figures shows the impact of the lower tax charge on purchased life annuities due to the exemption from tax of the capital element.

If the recipient is in a nursing home, tax can be avoided by arranging for the annuity to be paid directly to the home.

The best annuity rates can be found in weekend newspapers and the Annuity Bureau will help – ring (020) 7620 4090.

Income drawdown

It is no longer necessary to buy an annuity immediately on retirement. The decision can be deferred till any time up to reaching the age of 75. Clearly the longer you leave it the higher the rate should be and, meanwhile, your fund can continue to grow.

However, it is a requirement that some income be taken during the period of deferment and there are maximum and minimum amounts. This is called income drawdown.

> You can defer the purchase of an annuity till you reach 75, but there are minimum and maximum amounts to draw down in the period of deferment.

The amounts of drawdown are set by the government's Actuary's Department, the maximum being equivalent to the current best available standard single-life level annuity for your age at retirement and the minimum being 35% of that amount. They are then reviewed every 3 years, taking account of your age then.

If you die before buying the annuity, your heirs will receive the remaining capital sum less a 35% tax charge.

Experts tend to recommend that purchase of an annuity should not be deferred unless the fund exceeds £100,000 (some give an even higher figure), because there are substantial fixed costs involved.

> Because of the fixed costs involved, experts do not recommend income drawdown unless your fund exceeds £100,000.

It is not necessary to keep your fund with your investment provider; you can change to achieve better performance and/or administration, although there may be a charge to pay to your original provider as well as an initial charge to the new one. Try negotiating these down. The transfer can be to a self-invested pension plan (SIPP – see Chapter 5), as this gives you the choice of investment.

Once you have elected to take income drawdown you cannot make further contributions to your fund, but there is nothing to prevent you from paying into another pension fund, up to the age of 75, provided you have earnings or, even if not, into a stakeholder pension (see Chapter 3).

> Once you have elected to take income drawdown you cannot pay any more into that fund, but you can start another.

Maximum and minimum amounts

The following illustrates the current levels of maximum and minimum amounts of annual income drawdown, before income tax, based on an original pension fund of £100,000 from which 25% tax-free cash has been deducted, leaving £75,000 in the fund:

	Initial annual income	
	£	%
Male aged 55:		
maximum	7,200	9.6
minimum	2,520	3.3
Male aged 60:		
maximum	8,000	10.6
minimum	2,800	3.7
Male aged 65:		
maximum	9,100	12.0
minimum	3,200	4.3

(The amounts for females will be lower, due to longer life expectancy).

Depending on the rate of growth achieved by your fund, the minimum will more than preserve the value of the fund but the maximum is likely to reduce it.

> The minimum drawdown should ensure your fund will grow in value but the maximum is likely to reduce it.

Open annuity

This carries the income drawdown concept still further. The big advantage is that you are not obliged to buy an annuity at 75, although you may do so at any time and may be forced to if the value of the fund falls significantly. You can therefore keep the open annuity till your death, when the capital passes to your estate, where it is subject to inheritance tax.

There is still a minimum income (which is reviewed regularly in line with your age, annuity rates and the growth of your investments). This is likely to be higher than under the ordinary income drawdown arrangement. The pension fund must be invested in pooled funds such as unit trusts, which is more limiting than ordinary income drawdown.

> With open annuities you can defer the purchase of a normal annuity beyond the age of 75.

When to choose income drawdown

This may be suitable in any of the following circumstances:

- ♦ You are only partly retiring but require some initial income.

- You are retiring early and consider you can obtain a better annuity when you are older.
- You think you can obtain better returns than can be bought with an annuity.
- You have experience of investing your pension fund successfully as you are in an SSAS or SIPP (see Chapter 5).
- You wish to take tax-free cash whilst delaying purchase of an annuity.
- You wish to protect the majority of your pension fund for your heirs in case you die before 75, especially if you are in poor health (or till your death in the case of the open annuity).
- You require flexibility of income to deal with future expenses or windfalls (examples being a family wedding or maturing investments).

It may be dangerous to defer purchasing an annuity merely because rates are low – there is no reason for expecting them to rise and the likelihood is the downward trend will continue, due to increasing life expectancy.

> Annuity rates have fallen over recent years and are not likely to increase again.

Phased retirement

Another way of deferring the purchase of the full annuity is to take phased retirement. In this case the pension fund is divided into a number of portions and one portion is taken at a time. Each portion includes the relevant amount of tax-free cash and the balance of the portion is used to purchase an annuity. Meanwhile, the amount left in the fund continues to grow.

This method is most suitable for someone who continues to work part time but needs not only some income from the fund but also some tax-free cash.

Voluntary purchase

Should you use your tax-free lump sum (or part of it) to buy a purchased life annuity?

The decision very much depends on how well you can manage on your other income, including your remaining pension and state pension.

> If you will not be able to manage on your state pension and compulsory annuity, you should consider using your tax-free lump sum to buy a voluntary annuity.

It is likely you can get a higher return than from a deposit account but you have to remember the annuity dies with you. There is nothing left for your heirs unless you get capital protection, which will reduce the return. You may be prepared to aim for a higher return through taking more risk with your money, but many pensioners need income rather than capital growth, which is where higher returns generally come from.

In short, the decision about whether to buy a voluntary pension is partly an investment decision, and you may decide to ask for advice from an independent financial adviser.

Action points

- **If you have to buy an annuity with your pension money, give careful consideration as to which type of annuity is best for you.**

- **Shop around for the best rates currently available. Look in newspapers for an indication of what they should be for the type of annuity you have chosen (it might be a good idea to compare rates for different types before making the final decision).**

- **If you have a large fund available, consider deferring the purchase of the annuity, bearing in mind the maximum and minimum amounts you must draw down.**

- **Compare the purchase of a voluntary annuity with the other investments available to you, seeking advice if desirable. When comparing returns, remember the annuity normally dies with you.**

Chapter 5

Other Pension Formats

In this chapter:

- **executive pension plans (EPPs)**
- **small self-administered schemes (SSASs)**
- **self-invested personal pensions (SIPPs)**
- **funded unapproved retirement benefit schemes (FURBSs)**
- **pension mortgages**
- **pensions and divorce.**

This chapter explains certain specialised pension schemes, which mainly apply to higher-paid people. Also dealt with here are pension mortgages and the effect of divorce on pension entitlements.

Executive plans and small self-administered schemes are specialised forms of occupational pensions, EPPs for the higher-paid employees of larger companies and SSASs for the directors and/or owners of smaller companies or businesses. Self-invested personal pensions are a form of personal pension that permit self-control of investment. They are usually for highly paid people.

> The choice between EPPs, SSASs and SIPPs is not easy and expert help should be obtained.

Unapproved schemes are occupational schemes that fall outside the Inland Revenue limits, in particular in respect of the maximum permitted salary. Pension mortgages are more for people who have limited funds and wish to use them to save for a pension as well as buy a home. Recent legislation permits the splitting of pensions on divorce, which can be particularly useful to a spouse who has not been working.

Is this you?
- I am being promoted and have been offered membership of the company's executive scheme. Should I accept?
- As the owner of a business my accountant suggests I should have an SSAS but I am not sure as I do not understand what it means.
- I consider that I manage my investments pretty well and would like to take over the management of my personal pension investments. Is it allowed?
- Bonuses take my pay over £100,000 a year, which is more than the company pension scheme allows. How can I get a pension on the excess?
- I run a small business and funds are short but now I am getting married and need to save for a pension as well as take out a mortgage.
- I am divorcing my husband but I will lose any rights I might have had under his pension scheme. Can I do anything about it?

Executive pension plans (EPPs)

Companies frequently have separate schemes for directors and senior executives. They are still occupational schemes but, in the case of defined benefit schemes, may provide higher benefits than the main company scheme, with significantly higher company contributions.

It is possible to have separate categories of members in the main scheme but, especially with the requirement for greater provision of information to members and the involvement of employee trustees, some companies prefer to keep the details more confidential in a separate scheme.

All the statutory requirements for occupational schemes apply to executive schemes.

Self-investment can be achieved in an executive scheme by arranging for the insurer to loan back the funds, but self-investment is easier in an SSAS.

Sometimes these are single-member schemes and, if there are fewer than three members, there are fewer statutory restraints than with ordinary occupational pensions. But the limited price indexation (LPI) rule applies, which makes them less attractive compared to SIPPs, which are dealt with below. (LPI is full indexation up to 5% per annum, calculated on the retail price index, in respect of benefits earned after 6 April 1997.)

For larger groups of employees, group personal pension schemes (see Chapter 3) are an alternative to money-purchase occupational schemes for executives, especially since contributions can be more flexible. However, executive schemes, since they are occupational schemes, can offer significantly higher tax-free cash at retirement than is possible under personal pensions.

Relevant executive pension plans

This term describes executive pension plans where the members are either current or former directors and certain other requirements are met. The advantage is exemption from some of the minor requirements of the Pensions Act 1995.

Small self-administered schemes (SSASs)

SSASs are a specialised form of occupational pension. There can be no more than 12 members and usually there are far fewer, sometimes only one. To qualify, a scheme must have at least 10% of its assets invested in non-insured items.

The usual Inland Revenue rules apply (see Chapter 2), in particular the application of limited price indexation to benefits earned after 6 April 1997, which has constrained one of the advantages of SSASs – greater choice over the level of increases to pensions in payment.

> The introduction of limited price indexation has reduced the attraction of SSASs compared with SIPPs.

An advantage of SSASs is that purchase of an annuity can be delayed till age 75, as with personal pensions. However, there is a possibility this might be extended to all schemes at some time in the future.

SSASs (where all the members are trustees and certain other requirements are met) are exempt from certain minor requirements of the Pensions Act 1995, as are EPPs (see above).

Investing the funds

SSASs are particularly suitable for directors/owners of a business, as legislation permits wide investment freedom. In particular, investment in property is permitted – even the property occupied by the business. Also, the scheme can lend money to the company and, subject to meeting certain requirements, can invest in the company's shares.

This means an SSAS is a financial planning tool as well as a pension scheme. However, whilst very convenient in certain circumstances, self-investment of this nature is probably more risky than other investments. Diversification of investments as soon as possible should be the investment objective.

> An SSAS can be a financial planning tool for directors/owners of a business.

Also, property is relatively illiquid, so an SSAS may need to move to more liquid investments as members approach retirement. Cashflow forecasts are essential. If the member(s) do not require such freedom of investment, an EPP (see above) might be simpler, as less administration work is necessary.

Self-invested personal pensions (SIPPs)

SIPPs are a sophisticated form of personal pension where, instead of going to a pension provider to do all the work – in particular the investing – you choose to do it yourself. You do need to be sure you are capable of managing your own pension investments and, in addition, of carrying out the necessary administration. However, you can employ someone to do some of these things for you – for example, you can subcontract out the paperwork (there is less paperwork than with an occupational scheme). Also, you may feel you need some investment advice, at least to start with.

SIPPs are usually taken on only by someone who has (or will eventually have) a large fund to control, as there are still costs involved. In particular, the cost of setting up the scheme can be around £500 and annual charges at least half that amount. Many advisers suggest it is not worth while setting up a SIPP if your fund is below £100,000. Others point out that the costs compare favourably with the charges for a traditional personal pension.

SIPPs are now becoming available on the Internet, where fees are generally lower than the more traditional format. Also, administration is simpler. Another advantage is the 24 hour a day availability of information, particularly investment valuations.

The usual Inland Revenue rules for personal pensions (see Chapter 3) apply to SIPPs. In particular, after taking tax-free cash, funds must be used to buy an annuity (but this can be deferred till age 75 – see Chapter 4 under 'Income drawdown').

SIPPs are frequently split into a series of individual arrangements (sometimes as many as 1,000). This allows the member to buy an annuity with some, take tax-free cash with others and leave the remainder to accumulate.

SIPPs are worth considering by those who are attracted by the investment freedom but are not eligible for an SSAS. In any case, following the introduction of limited price inflation from 1997, those who are eligible for an SSAS may prefer to have a SIPP as they will have greater choice in the level of post-retirement increases.

Investing your SIPP
Legislation permits up to 25% of the fund to be held in cash form, although whether this is a good idea

(except when you expect the stock market to fall or when you are nearing retirement) is an investment decision. Generally, pension investment is long term, so you can take advantage of the much higher long-term growth rate of equities and ignore short-term falls in value. If you are a sophisticated investor, you can protect your fund against anticipated stock market falls by 'hedging' – selling options, for example, or using the growing spread-betting market.

> Above all, though, you do need to know how to invest wisely.

Also, investing monthly contributions means you can take advantage of 'pound-cost averaging' – a curious description of the phenomenon that, when the stock market is low, you get more shares or units for your monthly contribution than when it is high, so that the average price you have paid for each share or unit is less than the average of the prices at which you bought. In the long run, this can have a considerable impact.

Funded unapproved retirement benefit schemes (FURBSs)

A pension scheme is approved (by the Inland Revenue) if it meets all the criteria laid down, particularly the maximum limits for contribution and benefits. One particular area of relevance is where the pay of members exceeds the maximum permitted (currently

£97,200). The employer may consider it necessary to recruit and keep highly paid people by having an unapproved scheme in respect of the excess salary over the Inland Revenue limit.

The main impact on the company is that contributions are not an allowable deduction for income tax. The same thing would apply to members, but such schemes are frequently financed entirely by the company. Also, there is no tax-free cash on retirement. Benefits, whether from money purchase (the usual basis) or defined benefit, must be paid out in full and are subject to income tax.

Buy-to-let
If you are a higher-rate taxpayer and wish to invest in property over the medium to long term, a FURBS is a good way of financing the investment as there are savings on income and capital gains taxes and inheritance tax can be avoided. You finance the property purchase through a FURBS in a company you set up for the purpose. You will need enough cash to start off with to pay the 25% deposit. The pension scheme buys the property and your pension contributions finance the mortgage repayments.

> There are substantial costs involved in setting up buy-to-let arrangements, so this method is only suitable for people who can finance a large property portfolio.

There are significant tax advantages:

♦ Company profits are taxed at the favourable small company rate of 22%.
♦ The company pays a lower rate of capital gains tax (34%).
♦ Inheritance tax is avoided as the property passes to your heirs from the company and so stays out of your estate.

Pension mortgages

The lump sum entitlement on retirement under a personal pension scheme (but not an occupational scheme) can be pledged to pay off a mortgage loan.

> The lump sum from a company scheme can be used to pay off a mortgage.

The advantage is that this combination of pension and mortgage provides the lowest mortgage cost as the mortgage is on an interest-only basis. But there are a number of reasons for not doing it:

♦ There may not be enough money to pay off the loan when retirement comes.
♦ There is little or no lump sum on retirement to use for other things.
♦ You could be faced with a difficult choice if you change jobs to one where there is an attractive company pension scheme.

Pensions and divorce

Pensions have always been a bone of contention on divorce, particularly if one spouse has not been working and so has not earned a pension for him or herself. Before 1996, pensions were not included as an asset in a divorce settlement.

In 1996, 'earmarking' was introduced, whereby part of the eventual pension and/or the lump sum could be directed towards the ex-spouse. However, this was still unsatisfactory, since it did not come into operation until the pensioned spouse retired, which might be a considerable period ahead.

Starting in 2000, pension splitting is now possible. The pension rights earned by the spouse who is a member of a pension scheme (in the form of its capital value) can now be split between the two parties to the divorce. It applies to the state second pension as well as occupational, personal and stakeholder pensions. This allows the spouse without a pension to have a separate one, which can be taken according to the rules of the scheme. If more appropriate, the capital sum can be transferred to another scheme, in particular to a personal pension scheme.

Since the pension is only part of what needs to be taken into account on divorce (the other potentially high value item being the home), it does not follow that pension splitting will be the best solution in every case. However, it does widen the options substantially.

Pension earmarking and splitting only apply to married couples and not to 'common law' spouses.

Adequate professional advice is needed by both parties – separately. Those whose pensions are made inadequate by splitting need to recognise the importance of making up the difference.

Action points

- **If you have the opportunity to join your company's executive pension scheme, it probably pays to do so. See if the benefits are better than in the ordinary scheme.**

- **If you are the director/owner of a business and would like to access your pension scheme funds to invest in the business, get advice about starting an SSAS.**

- **If you have a personal pension and you are good at investing, get advice about switching to an SIPP.**

- **If your salary exceeds the approved occupational pension scheme maximum (currently £97,200), discuss with your employer the possibility of starting a FURBS.**

- If you are short of funds, you can combine your pension with your mortgage, thereby reducing the total payments, but get advice first.

- If you are getting divorced, and especially if you are a non-earner, get advice about whether pension splitting would be good for you.

Chapter 6

Retirement Planning

In this chapter:

- **other savings**
- **getting pension forecasts**
- **assessing your post-retirement position**
- **supplementing your income**
- **retiring early**
- **late retirement.**

Do not let retirement creep up on you without making preparations for it. You should be doing this at least 5 years ahead of your planned retirement date, which may be earlier than the statutory age (65 for men, 60 for women, at present).

Many people are saving surplus earnings and investing them with a view to providing additional income after retirement. You can get forecasts of your pension well in advance of retirement – state as well as occupational or personal. You need to assess your financial position after retirement to see whether further action is necessary, including supplementing your income.

There is a lot of planning to do and you may feel you need advice and help. Consider going to a pre-retirement class or get some literature – your employer might already be providing something.

Before retiring early, find out what the implications are. You may wish to defer retirement, either because you are fit and wish to carry on working or because you need to increase your income when you do retire.

> **Is this you?**
> ♦ I'm saving up for extra income in retirement but am not sure where to invest.
> ♦ How do I find out how much pension I will receive when I retire?
> ♦ Will I have enough to live on in my retirement?
> ♦ I'd like to retire early but don't know whether I can afford it.
> ♦ My employer wants me to carry on working after I reach my normal retirement date. How will this affect my pension?

Other savings

The best way to invest for retirement is through a pension scheme, but there are other investments that can be used for savings.

Pension contributions

The first step is to make sure you are using all your pension contribution rights. Have you any shortfall on the state basic pension you can make up with additional contributions (see Chapter 1)? If you have a company pension, are you making AVCs (see Chapter 2) to bring your contribution to the pension scheme up to the maximum of 15% of earnings? Similarly, with a personal pension, are you making the maximum contributions (see Chapter 3)? Finally, can you contribute to a stakeholder pension (see Chapter 3)?

ISAs

Next, you should consider tax-efficient investments, and the most important of these is the ISA (individual savings account). You can currently put up to £7,000 a year into an ISA account (and so can your partner). Once within the account, investments grow free of income and capital gains tax and, in retirement, you can withdraw income (or capital) to supplement your pension.

ISAs are not investments in themselves but 'wrappers' that can be placed around various types of investment in order to get tax advantages. So it is necessary to choose the type of investment you wish to make within the ISA.

You can put all the £7,000 annual investment in a stocks and shares maxi-ISA. If you wish to put up to the £3,000 allowed annually in a cash mini-ISA, the maximum you can put in a stocks and shares mini-ISA is also £3,000, the other £1,000 only being eligible for an insurance mini-ISA.

If you have over, say, 5 years to go before retiring, it is best to invest in equity-based products, such as unit trusts, investment trusts or even directly in equities if you think you have the necessary skills. This is because, over the longer term, they grow faster than fixed-interest investments.

As the need to use the investments for income nears, you should consider a gradual switch to fixed interest as you may otherwise be faced with a need to realise equities when the market is down. Investments in a stocks and shares ISA can be switched to fixed-interest products such as gilts (government fixed-interest stocks) and corporate bonds (company-fixed interest).

> The relative merits of ISAs and AVCs are discussed in Chapter 2.

PEPs and TESSAs

No new investments are permitted in these two tax-free items. However, existing investments in a PEP (personal equity plan, which is a wrapper like an ISA) can be retained. In the case of a TESSA (tax-efficient special savings account) the capital originally invested can, when the 5-year investment period is up, be transferred into a TESSA-only ISA without counting against that year's annual ISA allowance.

Other investments

National Savings

There are some fixed-interest investments that are tax efficient, such as National Savings certificates. There is full security of capital but, currently, the returns are not high (except for higher-rate income-tax payers). Your money is tied up for 3 or 5 years and the interest rate is fixed for that period, but cannot be accessed until expiry. Index-linked certificates, which pay a fixed rate of interest above retail price inflation, are a good way of conserving the real value of your investment and are particularly of interest to higher-rate taxpayers as the growth in value is tax free.

With-profits bonds

This is another favourite form of investment for pensioners or those nearing pension age. Whilst you need to invest for a minimum of 5 years to avoid early redemption charges, the value of the fund is unlikely to fall because annual bonuses are declared but some growth is retained to smooth out returns and to pay for terminal bonuses (payable on terminating the investment).

> With-profits bonds have become a very popular form of investment, particularly with retired people, probably because of their steadiness in growth, despite the disadvantage of not knowing in advance what the terminal bonus will be.

Income tax and capital gains tax are payable by the fund at the standard rate and no further tax is payable by standard-rate taxpayers. Tax deducted cannot be recovered, so they are not suitable for non-taxpayers. Higher-rate taxpayers will have to pay the extra 18% tax, but not until maturity, the advantage of the deferred tax being that the fund grows with only standard-rate tax having been deducted. If withdrawals are made before maturity, the additional tax is immediately payable unless the withdrawal is limited to 5% of the fund each year. The percentage is on a cumulative basis, so you can exceed 5% in a year if you withdrew less in earlier years.

On retirement, when your income generally falls, the marginal rate for some higher-rate taxpayers may no longer be above the standard rate band, so income can be taken without further income tax liability (unless it takes you back into the higher rate band). If you are saving significant amounts for supplementing your retirement income, you may consider seeking advice from an independent financial adviser.

Getting pension forecasts

Get a forecast of your state pension entitlement about 5 years before you intend to retire to see if you can get more by making additional contributions – ask your local DSS office for an application form. Shortly before retirement your occupational schemes normally provide a quote showing your pension and that is when you decide about taking a cash lump sum. But you can get information sooner if you need it – ask the scheme administrator.

Many employers offer pre-retirement courses and/or books or magazines. Take advantage of any such offers.

With a personal pension the provider will tell you the lump sum available and give an indication of annuity rates. This is when you decide whether to defer taking the pension.

Assessing your post-retirement position

Once you have obtained the pension forecasts, prepare an income and expenditure budget for after retirement. You must not forget to allow for the pension reduction from taking the tax-free lump sum, if that is what you intend to do. Remember that some expenses cease, such as the cost of travel to work (and the cost of prescriptions!), but do include in your budget the cost of additional holidays you may well take now that you have more time available.

Consider whether to use your lump sum to reduce or pay off any mortgage you still have. Otherwise, you may need to invest it to produce more income than it would have yielded if left in the scheme.

Bear in mind that inflation can reduce the real value of your pension. You may well have partial inflation-proofing but it might not be enough because, although inflation seems well under control at present (less than the watershed of 5%), you will hopefully be a long time retired.

A year or two before retirement review your investments to see if you should start switching from growth to income investments in order to supplement your income.

Supplementing your income

If, despite all these actions, you do think you are going to need more income in retirement, there are other more drastic steps to consider.

> Do take into account the minimum income guarantee (see Chapter 1). In view of the restrictions on savings in order to qualify for the guarantee, if your savings already exceed the minimum amount at which the cut-back starts (currently £6,000), it may well not be worth scrimping to save more.

Taking in lodgers or tenants

You can let furnished rooms in your home. Under the rent-a-room scheme, net income from such lettings is currently free of tax up to £4,250 a year (and there are concessions for income just over that amount). Expenses can be charged against gross income for tax purposes and you can increase income and charge more expenses if you feed your lodger as well.

There is a risk of incurring some capital gains tax on subsequent sale of the property. There are leaflets available from the Inland Revenue, and advice can be obtained from the Citizen's Advice Bureau.

Home equity release

These are schemes whereby elderly people can raise more income from their homes. The minimum age at which they become viable is 75, or combined ages of 160 for a couple.

> It is vital to get legal advice about home equity release schemes. In the past, some ruthless providers have attracted bad publicity for them, but they are now much more acceptable.

There are three kinds of home equity release schemes.

Home income plans

An interest-only mortgage is taken out and the amount borrowed is used to buy an annuity. Part of the annuity income is used to pay the loan interest and the balance is additional income. The mortgage is repaid from the proceeds of selling the home after the death of the occupant(s). To avoid uncertainty, a fixed-interest mortgage is desirable. Remember that income from the annuity is subject to tax only on the interest portion and then only at 20%.

Home reversion schemes

In this case part or all of the house is sold to an institutional investor for a proportion of the value, depending on the age of the seller. The buyer grants a free lease for the life of the seller.

Roll-up loans

A lump sum is borrowed and you do not have to repay capital or pay interest before your death, unless your loan plus interest outstanding exceeds a percentage of the house value (e.g. 75%). You therefore take the risk of an adverse movement of interest rates causing premature repayment. For this reason, roll-up loans are not recommended.

Retiring early

There are a number of issues to take into account if you are planning to retire early.

> If you wish to retire early, it is essential to take account of all the factors that can affect the pensions you receive.

State pensions

The earliest date you can start to draw the state basic and additional pensions is 65 for men, 60 for women. If you are a wife entitled only to the category B pension (see Chapter 1), even if you have reached state retirement age, you must wait until your husband on whose pension the B pension is based has reached the age of 65. But once he has reached that age, even if you are below 60, you can receive the pension.

Some occupational schemes have a normal retirement date earlier than the state pension age. You therefore need to take account of the lower total pension during the intervening period. Some such schemes offer a choice of using part of your fund value to finance a higher company pension during the period up to state pension age, to make up the difference, but afterwards the company pension will be lower.

Occupational pensions

Under Inland Revenue rules, early retirement on the grounds of ill-health can take place at any time but, otherwise, it is not permitted until you reach 50. Scheme rules are allowed to be narrower and frequently are in the case of defined benefit schemes, perhaps 55 for men (50 for women).

The amount of pension when retiring early under a defined benefit scheme is lower for two reasons: contributions are less and payment is likely to be for longer. The lower level of contributions means the accrued benefit is lower. The earlier payment of that benefit is usually taken care of by a formula (called the early retirement factor – ERF) based on the number of years and months actual retirement date precedes normal retirement date. A common ERF is 4% per annum, which means a reduction of 20% for retiring 5 years early.

In the case of early retirement due to ill-health, rules frequently provide for the ERF to be ignored. It is usually necessary for the scheme trustees to be satisfied you have a genuine case, perhaps by arranging for a medical with a nominated doctor.

Where a company wishes to encourage early retirement, the package may be made more attractive by removing the ERF but, in such cases, the scheme trustees will require the company to meet the cost by paying in a lump sum to make up for the ERF. The effect of early retirement from a defined contribution scheme is the same as for a personal pension (see below). However, the company can make additional contributions to provide a larger fund, if it wishes to encourage early retirement.

Personal pensions
The position under a personal pension is similar. The accrued pension fund will be lower due to fewer contributions and the annuity bought by the fund will also be lower because it starts at an earlier age. There is a possibility of additional company contributions to encourage early retirement but, in this case, only if there is room within the maximum permitted

contributions. In respect of ill-health early retirement, the only possibility for a higher post-retirement income arises if your health is so bad an impaired life annuity (see Chapter 4 under 'types of annuity') is possible.

Stakeholder pensions

The rules for early retirement are the same as for personal pensions.

Late retirement

State pensions

There is a formula for increasing state pensions if the starting date is deferred. It is increased by 7.5% for each year of deferment up to the age of 70. Although this sounds quite a high return, the calculation must take into account the pension you have not received and it takes 12 years to catch up.

Company pensions

Normally, contributions cease on reaching normal retirement age but drawing the pension can be deferred, perhaps up till the age of 75, if the scheme rules permit. In a defined benefit scheme the pension paid will take into account the additional years of service, so it will be higher. However, if the pension is based only on the final year's salary (or the average of the last 3 years) and you continue at work on a part-time basis at a lower salary, your pension will be lower.

If you have long service and a high accrual rate, remember your pension cannot exceed the Inland Revenue maximum of two thirds pensionable pay. However, that maximum can be calculated from the highest pay over 3 consecutive years in the last 10 before retirement, indexed by retail price inflation till retirement date, so it is unlikely to be exceeded.

In a defined contribution scheme the effect of late retirement will be the same as for a personal pension (see below).

Personal pensions

You can go on contributing up to the age of 75, and deferring purchase of your annuity means it will be higher when you do buy it.

> If you are planning to delay your retirement, you need to check the effect of postponement on all your pensions. It may well be you decide to take some or all of them at normal retirement date. In this connection, your marginal rate of income tax is a factor to take into account.

Action points

♦ **Can you save for your retirement to provide additional income then? Do you have existing investments that can be used for this purpose?**

- **Find out what your pensions are forecast to provide.**

- **If nearing retirement, have you prepared a post-retirement income and expenditure budget to see where you stand?**

- **If you need more income in retirement, consider ways of achieving it.**

- **Most people would like to retire early. If you are one, make yourself aware of the financial implications.**

- **You may wish (or need) to go on working after state pension age but, before you decide, take account of the impact on your pensions.**

Appendices

A Pension Regulatory Bodies

Financial Ombudsman Service (FOS)

If you have a problem with a personal pension and cannot resolve it, the FOS can help. This Ombudsman also deals with complaints about advice to transfer or opt out of a company scheme into a personal pension.

Occupational Pensions Advisory Service (OPAS)

This service becomes available if you have tried but failed to resolve a problem with your company pension scheme. It will:

- explain your benefits if you do not understand them;
- write on your behalf to the pension scheme to obtain more information; and
- take up with the scheme any lack of payment of benefits due to you.

It cannot arbitrate or instigate legal proceedings on your behalf but, in the event of failure to resolve an issue, will help you make a formal complaint to the Pensions Ombudsman.

Occupational Pensions Regulatory Authority (OPRA)

This body regulates occupational schemes and is responsible for maintaining law and order in the pensions world. It does not become involved in individual complaints but will listen to scheme members who are unhappy about the way the scheme is being run. It also listens to trustees, employers and professional advisers to a scheme, and by law, actuaries and auditors have a duty to tell OPRA if they find out the rules are being broken.

Pensions Compensation Board

They can step in and pay compensation where money has been taken dishonestly from a company pension scheme and the company is insolvent.

Pensions Ombudsman

The ombudsman will formally decide upon a complaint regarding an occupational scheme, that has not been resolved directly or by OPAS.

The Pension Schemes Registry

They can help you to trace a scheme you have money in but cannot find, so you can claim your rights.

Addresses and telephone numbers

Financial Ombudsman Service
South Quay Plaza
183 Marsh Wall
London E14 9SR
0845 080 1800

OPAS
11 Belgrave Road
London SW1V 1RB
0845 601 2923   www.opas.org.uk

OPRA
Invicta House
Trafalgar Place
Brighton BN1 4DW
01273 627 600   www.opra.gov.uk

Pensions Compensation Board
11 Belgrave Road
London SW1V 1RB
020 7828 9794

Pensions Ombudsman
11 Belgrave Road
London SW1V 1RB
020 7834 9144

Pensions Schemes Registry
PO Box 1NN
Newcastle upon Tyne NE99 1NN
0191 225 6393   www.opra.gov.uk

B Contribution conditions for the state basic pension

There are two conditions that must be met.

Condition 1

You must either:

- have one 'qualifying year' (see below) since 6 April 1975 as a result of paying class 1, 2 or 3 National Insurance contributions (NICs); or
- have paid 50 flat-rate contributions at any time before 6 April 1975.

If you receive a category B pension based on your spouse's contributions (see below), condition 1 applies to your spouse instead of to you.

Condition 2

To get the minimum amount of basic pension, which is 25% of the full rate, you need at least seven qualifying years. The actual minimum number of years you need depends on the length of your 'working life' (see below).

There is a table in the *Guide to Retirement Pensions* booklet that shows the minimum number of qualifying years applicable to the length of your working life. It also shows the percentage of the full rate you will receive, based on the length of your working life and the number of qualifying years you have.

> Check the table in the guide to find out what percentage of the full basic pension you should receive.

To get the full-rate basic pension you must have qualifying years for about 90% of your working life. The 10% shortfall allowed in your working life is applied as 5 years off a working life of 41 years or more, and 4 years off for a working life of 31–40 years.

Definition of working life

This is the period over which you have to meet the contribution conditions. It is counted from the start of the tax year in which you reach 16 to the end of the tax year before the one in which you reach pensionable age. (A tax year runs from 6 April one year to 5 April the following year.)

Your working life is therefore a maximum of 49 years for men. For women it is 44 years, increasing by one year if you were born between 6 October 1950 and 5 October 1951 and by one more year for each year after that, reaching 49 years if you were born after 5 October 1954.

> The maximum working life is 49 years for men and currently 44 years for women.

Definition of a qualifying year

A qualifying year is one in which you have received 'qualifying earnings' (see below) of at least 52 times the lower earnings limit (LEL) for that year (only 50 times in respect of the period from 6 April 1975 to 5 April 1978).

The LEL is the level of earnings above which NICs are paid. It increases each year, the current amount being £88.75 a week. (The upper earnings limit – UEL – is the level of earnings above which NICs are not paid or only 1% from April 2003.)

Men are credited with the final 5 qualifying years up to pensionable age. This will be extended to women in 2010, when their pensionable age has increased to 65.

> A qualifying year is one in which your earnings are at least 52 times the lower earnings limit for that year.

Definition of qualifying earnings

All your earnings each year count, including those on which you have paid full-rate class 1 (employee) NICs. But if you are a married woman or a widow, earnings on which you have paid reduced-rate class 1 NICs do not count. For class 2 contributions (for the self-employed) and class 4 (voluntary contributions), each contribution counts as one week of earnings, at the lower earnings limit.

If your earnings in any year do not reach the level needed to make it a qualifying year but you have been receiving relevant benefits, you will be credited with each week you have not worked and received benefits instead.